FATHERS TALKING

AN ANTHOLOGY

Aelred Squire

AN INVITATION TO SERIOUS SPIRITUAL BROWSING

CISTERCIAN STUDIES SERIES: NUMBER NINETY-THREE

FATHERS TALKING

FATHERS TALKING

AN ANTHOLOGY

Aelred Squire

Cistercian Publications
Kalamazoo, Michigan

1986

BR63

F29

1986

Available in Britain and Europe from

A. R. Mowbray & Co Ltd
St Thomas House   Becket Street
Oxford OX1 1SJ

Available elsewhere (including Canada) from the publisher

Cistercian Publications
WMU Station
Kalamazoo, Michigan 49008

*The editors of Cistercian Publications express their gratitude
to the Koch Foundation of Clearwater, Florida,
for help in bringing this manuscript to publication.*

*The work of Cistercian Publications is made possible in part
by support from Western Michigan University*

Library of Congress Cataloguing-in-Publication data

Squire, Aelred.
  Fathers talking.

  (Cistercian studies series ; no. 93)
  1. Christian literature, Early—Addresses, essays,
lectures.   I. Title.   II. Series.
  BR63.S68   1986   270.1   86-2620
  ISBN 0-87907-893-6
  ISBN 0-87907-993-2 (pbk.)

*Typeset by Gale Akins, Kalamazoo
Printed in the United States of America*

For Antoninus,
a loyal friend
in a new land

CONTENTS

Still bearing fruit when they are old,
still full of sap, still green
Psalm 91:15
(Grail Psalter)

INTRODUCTION

*C*HRISTIANS, and perhaps more particularly christian monks, have from the earliest times kept notes of convictions about their faith and way of life which seemed to them to be expressed in ways that made them a resource and point of return. The following pages are an anthology of some leaves from the notebook of one who happens to be a modern monk. Yet all the entries are chosen from talks addressed to Christians in general by men who came to be regarded as qualified teachers and representatives of their faith in the years of its primitive vigour. With one exception, they are bishops, in no sense remote from their people, many of whom had been baptized by them; men who might have said with St Paul, *Though you have countless guides in Christ, you do not have many fathers. For I became your father in Christ Jesus through the gospel.* (1 Cor 4:15) If, among those now formally recognized as Fathers of the Church, Origen is allowed some place, although suspected of doubtful orthodoxy in some of his views, this is because his mature preaching, unmistakably loyal in substance and intention, is characterized by an undivided ardour and clarity of insight that ensured for it at least a secret influence. There is nothing quite like it. In any case, it is not the purpose of these pages to provide a miniature introduction to the study of the Fathers of the Church. It is intended rather as an invitation to serious spiritual browsing.

Browsing, an art of the open-minded and open-hearted, implies chosen leisure, time taken and time given, even if only in short stretches. An anthology of this kind will mean for many a notable change of pace, if it is to be used with pleasure and profit. For it must be remembered that each piece translated here from Latin or Greek was originally designed to be heard, rather than read with the eye, and that each seeks to engage a listening ear, capable of catching the hints and echoes of which all are full. Augustine does in fact speak differently when he means to be read. When speaking, he and the other Fathers in this collection intend to win the attention, not of specialists or theologians, but of the people of varied attainments who had become, or were becoming, members of the christian Church at a time when it was still surrounded, as it is once again, by many for whom the basic convictions of Christianity were profoundly alien. This was still true to some extent even of Gregory the Great, the latest of the Fathers to be quoted here, the language of one of whose passages may sound to those who know about these things already characteristically medieval. Yet none of these men shows any sign of preaching or recognizing what may be called a second-class Christianity. Whatever their recognition of human weakness, their unambiguous message to everyone is still the full claim of the gospel as they understand it. They suppose in their hearers only a growing knowledge of the text of the scriptures of the Old and New Testaments, as read or sung in the Church's liturgy; and the less one is cumbered by any theories about these, or about the Fathers themselves, the more accessible their words are likely to seem.

This conviction led me many years ago to illustrate my attempts to discuss the Fathers as transmitters and exponents of christian doctrine with translations of pieces of their works which were neither paraphrases nor contrived examples of archaic voices from the past. I soon found, contrary to what my elders and betters had assured me would be the case, that these pieces often excited my hearers as much as they had excited me, and that they served much better as communications of thought and feeling than dull abstracts dubiously claiming to convey the same ideas would have done. The poet Dylan Thomas remembered how in the chapel country of his native Wales a man of an older generation might think it appropriate to read his Bible wearing a bowler hat, and there still seem to be teachers who imagine that ordinary people cannot be exposed to the Fathers of the Church without the protection of a suitable covering, or some token of respect and distance. An authentic respect is, naturally, always fitting, yet those whom the common tradition of the undivided Church regards as its Fathers in the faith were never in their own day commissioned to play any such role. Their authority is ultimately based on the self-evident integrity of faith lived and loved. Nevertheless some scholars, anxious in case the role of patristic authority should be exaggerated or misconceived, will hasten to remind us that the works of the Fathers as a whole are by no means all sweetness and light, and that they also often knew a great deal less about the texts on which they were commenting than some of us do today. Such reserves must be allowed their measure of truth. Yet the broad vision of these men often has the unmistakable freshness and clarity of waters near their source—a privilege of time and place—and their limitations no more disqualify them from expressing convictions which can be soundly based on a view of the New Testament as a whole than the writers of the New Testament itself are disqualified for often seeing meanings in the Old Testament texts which can hardly have been clearly formed in the minds of those who originally wrote them.

Here, then, is a selection of Church Fathers talking to ordinary people about some of the things nearest to their hearts. The shape which seems to have emerged has surprised me as much as it will perhaps surprise some of my readers, even a few of the scholars among them. Leaving aside the two end-pieces from Origen and Augustine, who would have expected Leo the Great to find so prominent a place here? Read superficially, he can sometimes sound orthodox and dull. Yet no one in the West holds so firmly in his hand the essential threads of the fundamental doctrine of the image of God in human beings and its consequences for the life of the spirit. And perhaps no one in the East expressed so simply the dynamism of that doctrine in something like the language of a catechesis with undeniable roots in the New Testament, and innocent of a philosophical overlay. Among Leo's sermons no other themes occupy, even physically, so large a place as these—not even his view of the special claims of his own see, for which he has almost exclusively been known and quoted in more recent centuries. Woven together as this teaching is with an equally firm doctrine of the divine initiative in the gift of grace, rooted in the conviction of the first letter of John that 'God loved us first', paragraphs from Leo's sermons provide a natural frame within which to see the function of human initiative in the life of moral effort and prayer as suggested in the thought of Gregory the Great, and in the constant preoccupation of Augustine with the profound subject of conversion. Cyril of Jerusalem provides a suitable complement from the East of the kind of catechesis in which the mystery of the divine gift holds a prominent place. It would be possible to complain that the East should have been more generously represented in a book like this, yet I take leave to doubt whether it could have been done more simply and directly, and whether the result could so adequately have represented the teaching of the undivided Church. I believe that, taken together, these texts amount to a very simple instruction in the ideals and aspirations of the christian life, closely related to the great christian mysteries as understood in patristic times. I would not claim that this doctrine is directly 'mystical' in some technical sense of that word, but it would certainly be normal, as the experience of centuries has shown, that anyone honestly reflecting on it and living it out would find that it disposes and leads to a life of prayer and contemplation. I must, however, leave it to my readers, both the more and the less learned, to spell out the implications of what they will read here, holding as I do that the Fathers themselves are really their own best interpreters. I should prefer that my words not intrude upon theirs.

Naturally, everyone has a right to know what I have done with the texts that have come down to us. I hope I have provided sufficient indications of this in the notes set out at the end of this book, for those who will want them. The titles of the sections are often suggested by a phrase, and always by the content, of the passages quoted. Of translations, as of tastes, it is wiser not to dispute. I would only claim that mine aim at being translations and, wherever possible, their continuity is that of the original, though occasionally I have swept away subsidiary thoughts which might have hindered the appreciation of the main theme. Occasionally, too, I have combined paragraphs that in the original stood some distance apart. Early christian congregations were, I believe, substantially more robust than most of those even of my own boyhood, and in any case both Cyril and Augustine often mention how lengthy they themselves could be. Their congregations largely stood through sermons it is perhaps easier to savour seated on a chair, or even sitting up in bed, provided we lend our minds to them. I believe that many will find that they still deserve our attention, and discover that they rise from them with lighter and more confident hearts.

Camaldolese Hermitage,
Big Sur, California

AELRED SQUIRE, OSB *Cam.*

I

REBECCA
AT THE WELL[1]

REBECCA, says the Scripture, *came to draw water at the spring with the daughters of the city.*[2] Every day Rebecca came to the wells, daily she drew water. And because she was there at the wells every day, it was easy for her to be found by Abraham's servant and joined in marriage to Isaac.

Do you suppose these are mere diversions and tales the Holy Spirit tells you in the Scriptures? This is instruction for souls and spiritual teaching which forms and teaches you to come daily to the wells of the Scriptures, to the waters of the Holy Spirit and always to draw and take a full pitcher home, as holy Rebecca did. In no other way could she have been joined to a patriarch like Isaac who was *born of promise,*[3] except by drawing the waters and drawing so much of them that she could give drink not only to the family at home, but also to Abraham's servant—and not the servant only. The waters she drew were so abundant that she could supply the camels too, *until they had finished drinking,*[4] it says.

They are all mysteries, the things that are written. Christ wishes to espouse you too. For it is to you that he speaks by the prophet when he says: *I will betroth you to me for ever; I will betroth you to me in faith and mercy, and you shall know the Lord.*[5] And it is because he wishes to espouse you to himself that he sent his servant to you ahead of him. This servant is the prophetic word. Unless you receive it, you cannot be wedded to Christ.

Yet you must know that no one untrained and inexperienced receives the prophetic word, but only someone who knows how to draw water from the depths of the well, and enough of it to supply those who seem to be unreasoning and misguided—represented by the camels—that he may say that he is a *debtor to the wise and to the foolish.*[6]

In short, this is what that servant had said of himself: *Of the girls who come to the water, whichever says to me 'Drink, and I will water your camels', she shall be the bride of my master.*[7] Thus it was, then, that Rebecca, whose name means 'patience', lowered the pitcher on her shoulder when she saw the servant and pondered the prophetic word. But possibly you will say, if the servant stands for the prophetic word, how is it that he is refreshed by Rebecca, when it is rather *he* who should have refreshed *her?*

See, then, whether the prophetic word is not perhaps like the Lord Jesus. While being himself the bread of life and the one who feeds hungry souls, he admits that he is hungry when he says: *I was hungry and you fed me.*[8] Again, though himself living water[9] giving drink to everyone, he says to the Samaritan woman: *Give me a drink.*[10] Thus the prophetic word also gives drink to the thirsty, and yet is itself also said to be refreshed—as though it were thirsty—when it receives the dedicated effort and attention of those who study it. One of these is the kind of soul of which we are speaking. It does everything patiently and is so eager and elated by study like this that from its depths it is accustomed to draw the waters of knowledge. One of these is fit to be married to Christ.

And so, unless you come daily to the wells, unless every day you draw the waters, you will not only be unable to refresh others. You will yourself also suffer from a *thirst for the word of God.*[11] Hear the Lord, also, saying in the gospels: *If anyone thirsts, let him come to me and drink.*[12] But it seems to me that you do not *hunger and thirst for righteousness.*[13] How then will you be able to say: *As the deer longs for the fountains of water, so my soul longs for you, O God. My soul thirsts for the living God, when shall I come and appear before his face?*[14]

Come, then. Let us also, while we have time, drink of the well of vision where Isaac walks, and where he goes out to reflect.[15] Notice how many things happen at the waters to invite you, too, to come daily to the waters of the Word of God, and be present at his springs like Rebecca.

ORIGEN

II

AFTER HIS IMAGE[1]

*J*F WE LOYALLY and wisely weigh our original condition, beloved, we shall discover that human beings were made after the image of God, that we might be imitators of our maker. And this is the natural dignity of our kind that, in us, as in a mirror, the character of the divine kindness should shine out. It is to this, indeed, that the grace of our Saviour daily brings us back, when that which fell in the first Adam is raised up in the second.[2] Now the cause of our recovery is nothing other than the mercy of God, whom we would not love unless he first loved us and dispelled the darkness of our ignorance by the light of his truth. The Lord, foretelling this by the holy Isaiah says: *I will lead the blind in a way they did not know, and I shall make them tread paths they have not known. I will turn the darkness before them into light, and make the rough places into level ground.*[3] And again: *I was found by those who did not seek me, and I appeared to those who did not ask for me.*[4] How this was fulfilled the apostle John teaches us, saying: *We know that the Son of God has come and has given us understanding, to know him who is* *true; and we are in him who is true, in his Son.* And again: *And so we love, because God first loved us.*[5] Thus, by loving us, God remakes us after his image. And that he might find in us the character of his goodness, he gives us further the capacity to do what he does, lighting lamps in our souls, and enkindling us with the fire of his love that we may love, not only him, but whatever he loves. For if, between human beings, it is in the long run a similar way of living that makes a friendship solid,[6] it also happens that a taste for similar things often leads to base attachments. How much, then should we desire and endeavour not to differ in anything from what pleases God. Of this the prophet says: *There is wrath in his displeasure, and life in his will.*[7] For the nobility of the divine majesty cannot otherwise be found in us than by the likeness of our will to his.

And so, when our Lord says: *You shall love your God with all your heart, and with all your soul, and your neighbour as yourself,*[8] let the faithful soul receive the unfading love of its Creator and Ruler, and submit itself entirely to his will. For his works and decrees are never lacking in the truth of justice and the mercy of kindness. And if anyone should be burdened with great labors and countless difficulties, they will find a good reason to bear with them if they understand that they are either set right by obstacles, or tested by them. But our devotion to this love will never be perfect unless our neighbour is also loved. And by this word *neighbour* we are to understand not only those who are bound to us by ties of friendship or blood, but absolutely every human being with whom we share a common nature, whether they be enemies or companions, free or enslaved. For one Maker made us, and one Creator breathed life into us. We all have the benefit of the same sky and air, the same days and nights. And, although some are good and some are bad, some upright and others not, still God is generous to everyone, kind to all, as the apostles Paul and Barnabas told the Lycaonians, when speaking of God's providence: *In past generations he allowed all nations to walk in their own ways; yet he did not leave himself without witness, for he is good, and gave you from heaven rains and fruitful seasons, satisfying your hearts with food and gladness.*[9] But the wideness of christian grace has given us even stronger reasons for loving our neighbour. Stretching out to every part of the entire world, it despairs of no one, and teaches that no one should be passed over. And rightly does it also tell us that enemies are to be loved and persecutors prayed for. For, as it daily grafts branches of wild olive from every nation into its holy olive-tree, it makes friends of enemies, adopted children of strangers, and justified people out of sinners so that *at the name of Jesus every knee should bow, in heaven and on earth and under the earth, and every tongue confess that Jesus Christ is Lord, to the glory of God the Father.*[10]

LEO THE GREAT

III

CLAIMING OUR HONOR[1]

*Y*ES' THE ANGEL proclaims the birth of a king, and choirs of angels accompany his voice. Rejoicing together they cry: *Glory to God in the highest, and on earth peace to men of good will.*[2] Now, before our Redeemer was born in the flesh, we were at variance with the angels, from whose light and purity we were far distanced as a result of the first sin, and of daily sinning. For because, through sinning, we became strangers to God, God's citizens, the angels, regarded us as strangers to their company. Yet seeing that we recognized our king, his fellow citizens, the angels, recognized us again. Now that the king of heaven has taken the earth of our flesh, this angelic aristocracy no longer looks down on our weakness. They have returned to peace with us, and put behind them the reason for the earlier disagreement. They now respect as their colleagues those on whom, at one time, they had looked down as weak and degraded. This is why Lot and Joshua venerated angels and were not forbidden to do so. Yet, when John in his Apocalypse would have bowed down before an angel, that same angel restrained him from any need to do so, saying: *You must not do that. I am a fellow servant with you and your brethren.*[3] Before our Redeemer came, angels were venerated by human beings and the angels held their peace. Why should this be if the reason is not that our nature, which they once despised, is later taken above them, so that they tremble to see it lying prostrate at their feet? Nor dare they despise what is beneath them as weak, when they venerate it above them in the king of heaven. They do not feel contempt for a human being as a colleague when they adore, above them, a man who is God.

So then, beloved brothers and sisters, let us be careful that no unseemliness degrades us—seeing that, in the eternal foresight, we are both citizens of God and equals of his angels. Let us lay claim to our honor by the way we live. Let no immorality stain us, no shameful thought accuse us, no evil intent plague our minds, none of the rust of envy eat into us, no conceit puff us up, no ambition weaken us with earthly beckonings, no anger set us on fire. For human beings are called gods.[4] Be answerable for yourself, then, against the vices for the honor of God since, for your sake, God became man.

GREGORY THE GREAT

IV

LIGHTS
IN THE WORLD[1]

*E*VERYTHING THAT BELONGS to genuine love—
something we also, according to the Lord's prayer,
owe our enemies—should be our desire and aim. For the life
of reliable people should be of service not to themselves
alone but also to others, so that what we cannot do for them
by our words they may gain by our way of living. And so,
beloved, bearing in mind the unspeakable generosity of the
divine gifts towards us, let us be fellow-workers with the
grace of God working in us. For the kingdom of heaven does
not come to those who sleep, nor is lasting bliss poured out
upon those who are sunk in idleness and sloth. And because,
as the Apostle says, *if we suffer with him we shall also be
glorified with him,*[2] we must take that way which the Lord
himself *is,* as he tells us. Without anything of value to plead
for us, he helped us by his grace and by his example: by the
one healing those he called to adoption, by the other training
them for effort. But this work, beloved, is not only neither
rough nor burdensome for dutiful children and good servants.
It is actually easy and light. As our Lord says: *Come to me*

all who labor and are heavy laden, and I will give you rest. For my yoke is easy and my burden light.[3] So nothing is difficult, beloved, for those who are humble, or rough for those who are gentle.

Now in all these matters the thing which is always there is the kindness of God towards everyone. To no one does he deny his mercy, for he bestows so much upon everyone without discrimination, and prefers to offer his blessings to those whom he would be justified in punishing. What profit, what use is there in ceaselessly longing for things that have to be left behind us, even if they do not desert us first? Let our love for all that disappears be carried over to things that never wear out. Let the soul that is called to higher things find its pleasure in those of heaven. Strengthen your friendship with the holy angels. Enter the city of God which is promised us for a dwelling-place. Join the company of the patriarchs, the prophets, the apostles, and the martyrs. Let what makes them happy be a joy to you. Long for the things that enrich them, and seek their support by a true rivalry. For we shall share the same esteem as those whose company in dutifulness we keep. And so, while time is granted you to keep the commandments of God, *glorify God in your body* and shine, beloved, *like lights in the world.*[4] Let the lamps of your spirits always be burning, and let nothing dark establish itself in your hearts. For, as the Apostle says: *You were once dark, but now you are light in the Lord. Walk as children of light.*[5] And then, in you, will be fulfilled the likeness of the Wise Men who went before you. Thus will you *let your light shine before men that, seeing your good works, they may glorify your Father who is in heaven.*[6] For just as it is a grave deviation that among people by and large the name of the Lord should be blasphemed on account of bad Christians, so it is a great work of fidelity that his name should be praised for his servants' holy way of life.

LEO THE GREAT

V

LAZARUS, COME OUT![1]

ANYONE WHO HEARS MY WORD and believes in him who sent me, has eternal life.[2] Surely he did not want us to hear his word, and then not understand it? Since there is eternal life in hearing and believing, there is much more in understanding. Yet faith is a step towards religion, and the mature result of faith is understanding, so that we may reach eternal life, where the gospel is not read to us. And he who now provides us with the gospel will take away all forms of reading and the voices of the reader and preacher and, to all those who are his, he himself will appear; he cleansing them and giving them light, and they living and seeing that *in the beginning was the Word, and the Word was with God.*[3] Let us, then, turn our attention to who we are, and think about who it is we are hearing. Christ is God, and he is speaking with human beings. He wishes to be understood, and he will make them capable of it. He wishes to be seen, and he will open their eyes. Yet he speaks to us for no other reason than because what he promises is true.

He himself now explains it, and he goes on to say:

Truly, truly, I say to you, the hour is coming, and now is.
What could be clearer? From this point he really discloses
what he was saying, for now that very thing to which Christ
invites us occurs. *The hour is coming, and now is.* Which
hour? *When the dead will hear the voice of the Son of God,
and those who hear will live.*[4] What are we to suppose, my
brothers and sisters? Are there no dead people among the
mass of you who are listening to me? Those who believe and
act in the light of genuine faith are, indeed, living and not
dead. But those who do not believe, or believe like the devils,
as they tremble and live badly,[5] should more suitably be
counted as being dead. Yet this *hour* is still going on. For the
hour of which our Lord is speaking is not one of those that
go to make up the twelve hours of a single day. This is why,
from the time these words were spoken, until this very
moment, and until the end of time, this one hour continues.
Of this hour, John said in his letter: *Children, it is the last
hour.*[6] And so it is *now.* Let anyone who is alive, live—and
anyone who was dead, live. Let anyone who lay dead, hear
the voice of the Son of God, and rise and live. Our Lord
cried out with a loud voice at the tomb of Lazarus, and the
man who had been dead four days, rose. The one who was
rotting came out into the air. He was buried, with a stone
placed over him, but the voice of the Saviour split the resis-
tance of the rock. Is your heart so hard that the divine voice
does not yet break into it? Rise up within your heart, and
come out of your tomb. For anyone who believes, rises;
anyone who professes faith, comes out.

*The hour is coming and now is, when the dead shall hear
the voice of the Son of God, and those who hear will live.*
What will be the source of their life? Life itself. And which
life? The life of Christ. How do we know that it is the life of
Christ? *I am,* he says, *the way, the truth, and the life.*[7]
Would you like to walk? *I am the way.* Would you like not to
be deceived? *I am the truth.* Would you like not to die?
I am the life. All this your Saviour says to you. There is

nowhere to go, but to me; no way to go there, but through me. So that *hour* is going on now, and this is also quite clearly happening and it will absolutely never stop. People who were dead, rise and enter into life.

I may add something else on this subject which is perhaps clearer. Somebody lights a lamp. As far as the little flame that burns in it is concerned, its fire has its own light in itself. But when there was no lamp there, your eyes were useless and saw nothing. Now they have a light, but it is not their own. Likewise, if they turn away from the lamp, they are in the shadows; if they turn to it, they become light. Now, as long as the flame is burning, it gives light. If you wish to take away its light, you must also put it out, for it cannot be there and not be light. Yet Christ is a light that cannot be put out and, everlasting with the Father, is always bright, always shining, always burning. But you, in your sin, were cold. In your sin, you were dark. You turn to him to be made light. For the Apostle says: *Once you were darkness, but now you are light in the Lord.*[8] When he said: *Now you are light,* he added, *in the Lord.* In you, then, darkness, but light in the Lord. Why light? Because, by sharing in his light, you are light. But if you go away from the light that gives you light, you return to your darkness. Not so Christ, not so the Word of God. And how is this? *As the Father has life in himself, so he has granted the Son also to have life in himself.*[9] And as he has, so he gives.

AUGUSTINE OF HIPPO

VI

FRIENDS OF GOD[1]

S EEING THAT SACRED revelation abounds with the commands of the Lord, why is it that Our Lord says of love, as of a single command: *This is my commandment that you love one another?*[2] Unless it be that every command is concerned with love alone, and all are one commandment, since whatever is commanded is grounded in love alone. For, just as the many branches of a tree grow out of a single root, so the many virtues spring from one love, and the branch of a good deed is without a touch of green if it is not rooted in love. And so the commands of the Lord are many, and yet one—many in the different things to be done, one in the root of love. Now how this love is to be maintained he himself suggests when, in various things he says in Holy Scripture, he tells us that our friends are to be loved *in* him, and our enemies *for* him. His love is genuine who loves his friend in God, and his enemy for him. Yet there are not a few people who love their nearest with the tie of familiarity and blood—a kind of loving which is not in contradiction with holy writ. But what we offer by the impulse of nature is not the same as what we owe out of obedient love by the command of the Lord. Hence, when our Lord says, *This is my commandment that you love one another,* he immediately adds, *As I have loved you.* It is as though he were to say more clearly: Love for that reason for which I have loved you.

There is only one supreme proof of love, and that is if we love someone who is against us. This is why Truth himself endured the suffering of the cross and yet also offered his persecutors the sign of love, saying, *Father, forgive them, for they know not what they do.*[3] What is so surprising in the fact that, while they are alive, his disciples should love their enemies, when their master loved them when he was killed? He expressed the sum-total of love when he added: *No one has greater love than this that they should lay down their lives for their friends.*[4] Our Lord came to die for his enemies as well, and yet he spoke of laying down his life for his friends, thereby showing us that, since we can draw profit from loving our enemies, even those who persecute us are actually friends.

But just now no one is hounding us to death. How then shall we know whether we love our enemies? Yet there is something which should be done while the Church is at peace which will make it clear whether, in time of persecution, we shall be able to die for love. John clearly says the same thing: *If anyone has this world's goods and sees his brother in need, yet closes his heart against him, how does God's love abide in him?*[5] John the Baptist also says: *He who has two coats, let him share with him who has none.*[6] How shall anyone who, in time of peace, will not give his coat for God's sake, come to lay down his life in time of persecution? Therefore, that the virtue of love may be undefeated in time of trouble, it must be nourished by mercy in times of peace, so that someone may first learn to offer his possessions to almighty God and, finally, himself.

There follows: *You are my friends.* How great is the mercy of our Creator! We are unworthy servants, and yet we are called friends. How great an honor it is for human beings to be the friends of God. But having heard of the proud distinction, learn also of the hardship of the struggle for it: *If you do what I command you.* It is as though he said: You are delighted about the final outcome. Weigh well the efforts by which it is reached. *No longer do I call you servants, for the servant does not know what his master is doing; but I have called you friends, for all that I have heard from my Father I have made known to you.*[7] What are all the things he has heard from his Father, which he wished to make known to his servants in order to make them his friends, if they are not the joy of interior love, if they are not those festivals of the heavenly country which he daily impresses upon our minds by the longing of his love? For when we love these heavenly things of which we hear, we already know what we love, for the love itself is the knowledge.[8] And so he made all these things known to those who, turned away from earthly desires, were burning with torches of the highest love. It was these friends of God the prophet beheld when he said: *To me your friends, O God, are very dear.*[9] For a friend is said to be like a keeper of one's soul.[10] And so, because the psalmist foresaw God's chosen ones as separated from the love of this world and keeping the will of God in his heavenly commands, he admired them as the friends of God. They can be killed, and they refuse to waver. Look out over the whole world, my brothers and sisters, it is full of martyrs, witnesses of the truth. Therefore those numbered by God are many more than the sands to us. For how many there are, we cannot grasp.

GREGORY THE GREAT

VII

THE CHRIST OF THE PSALMS[1]

NOW YOU, says the Apostle, *are the body of Christ, and individually members.*[2] If then he is the head and we the body, one human person speaks. Whether it is the head that speaks or the members, it is the one Christ who speaks. And it is normal for the head to speak also for the members of the body. Notice our habits in this matter. For sometimes we have to say words in which there is nothing personal to us, but which only refer to our head. Yet he does not distinguish between our words and those which he uses of himself, and he will return from his words to ours. For of him and the Church it is said: *They shall be two in one flesh.*[3] These ideas are not new, you have always heard them. Yet from time to time it is necessary for them to be remembered.

I have called to you, Lord. Only hear me![4] This is something we can all say. I do not say this by myself. The whole Christ says it. But it is more particularly said in the name of the body. For when he was here and bore our flesh he prayed, and prayed to the Father in the name of the body and, while he prayed, drops of blood flowed from his whole body. So it stands in the gospel. Jesus prayed an urgent prayer and sweated blood.[5] What is this flow of blood from the whole body if it is not the suffering of the martyrs of the entire Church? *I have called to you Lord, Only hear me! Hear the voice of my prayer when I cry to you.* You supposed the business of crying out was over when you were saying, *I have called to you.* You have called. Do not yet be too reassured. If the trouble is over, the calling out is over. But if the trouble of the Church and the body of Christ continues until the end of the world, it not only says: *I have called to you, Only hear me!,* but also: *Hear the voice of my prayer when I cry to you.*

Let my prayer be set forth in your sight like incense; the raising of my hands like an evening sacrifice.[6] This is usually understood of the head himself, as every Christian knows. For as the day was drawing towards evening our Lord on the cross laid down his life to take it again; he did not lose it against his will. And yet we too are symbolized here. For what was it that hung upon the tree but what he took from us? And how could it ever come about that the Father should leave and abandon his only Son, who was indeed one God with him? Yet still, fastening our weakness to the cross, where, as the Apostle says, *our old human nature was fastened to the cross with him,*[7] with the voice of our own human nature he cried out: *My God, my God, why have you forsaken me?*[8] This then is the evening sacrifice, the passion of the Lord, the Lord's cross, the offering of the saving victim, the sacrifice pleasing to God. In his resurrection he made the evening sacrifice into a morning oblation. And so prayer, going up pure from a faithful heart, rises like incense from a holy altar. There is nothing more delightful than the fragrance of the Lord. May all who believe breathe out that fragrance.

I am alone until I pass over.[9] This phrase is said in the name of the head. In your passion you alone suffer, you alone are killed by your enemies. What then is the meaning of *until I pass over?* The Evangelist says: *When the hour had come for Jesus to pass out of this world to the Father.*[10] And so, until I pass over, I am alone. When I have passed over I shall become more. Many will imitate me, many suffer in my name. Hear the mystery of his words. In the Hebrew language, as those who know it translate it, the word *pascha* means 'a passing over'. And so, after Easter, I shall not be alone. After the 'passing-over' I shall not be alone. What is it that our Lord says in the psalm? *I am alone until I pass over.* If we have understood this phrase, remember his words in the gospel: *Truly, truly, I say to you,* he says, *unless a grain of wheat falls into the earth and dies, it remains alone; but if it dies, it bears much fruit.* He says this in the same place as he says: *When I am lifted up from the earth I will draw all things to myself.*[11]

AUGUSTINE OF HIPPO

VIII

FELLOW-
TRAVELLERS [1]

*E*VERY ACTION OF CHRIST is the glory of the
Church Catholic, but the glory of glories is the cross.
I admit to the cross, because I am certain of the resurrection.
If he had remained the crucified one, I should, perhaps, not
have spoken of it, but have drawn the veil over it and my
master. But knowing that the resurrection followed the cross,
I am not ashamed to tell of it.

Of the robbers crucified with him, it was said: *And he was
numbered with the transgressors.*[2] And before this, the two
were indeed transgressors. But one of them ceased to be. For
in fact, one was a transgressor, to the end refusing salvation
and, though his hands were fastened, he hit out with his
tongue in blasphemies. Jews who were passing by wagged
their heads, mocking the crucified one, and fulfilling what
was written: *When they see me they wag their heads.*[3] And
one of those with him did the same. But the other reproached
the one who was cursing. And for him it meant both the end
of life and the beginning of getting better, the surrender of
his soul and a foretaste of his salvation. And, after his

reproach of the other one, he said: *Lord, remember me.*
For it is to you I am speaking. Let him be, for the eyes of his
understanding are blinded. But, remember me. I do not say:
Remember the things I have done, for of those I am afraid.
Any human being is kindly disposed towards his fellow-
traveller. I am your companion on the way to death.
Remember me, your fellow-traveller. But I do not say:
Remember me *now. Remember me* rather, *when you come
into your kingdom.*[4]

O thief, what power gave you this light? Who taught you
to venerate the despised and crucified man at your side? O
eternal light, which enlightens those who lie in darkness! And
therefore it was right that he should hear: Be comforted. Not
that your doings should be the cause of your comfort, but
because the King is here to be gracious to you. What you ask
is a long way from what you need, but grace is very swift.
Truly, I say to you, today you will be with me in paradise,[5]
because today you have heard my voice and have not
hardened your heart.[6] I quickly passed sentence on Adam.
As quickly do I pardon you. For he was told: *In the day that
you eat of it, you shall die.*[7] But today you have lent your
ear to the faith, today means salvation for you. He fell by
the tree, and the tree will bring you into paradise. Do not fear
the serpent. He will not cast you out, for he has fallen from
heaven. And I do not say: Today you shall depart, but Today
you shall be with me. Be comforted; you shall not be cast
out. Do not fear the flaming sword; it respects its master.
Great and indescribable grace! The faithful Abraham has not
yet gone in, and the thief has entered. Not yet Moses and the
prophets, and the thief who breaks the law gets in. It was
before you that Paul was astounded when he said: *Where sin
increased, grace abounded all the more.*[8] Those who have
borne the heat of the day have not yet entered, but the one
who came about the eleventh hour has got in.[9] Let no
one grumble at the householder when he says: *Friend, I am
doing you no wrong. Am I not allowed to do what I choose*

with what belongs to me?[10] The robber would like to do things that are right, but death cuts him short. I am not concerned with works alone, but faith I will accept. I have some who feed my sheep among the lilies. I have some who feed them in the gardens. I have found the sheep that was lost and take it upon my shoulders. For he believes, since he has said: *I have gone astray like a lost sheep.*[11] *Remember me Lord, when you come into your kingdom.*

In the Canticle I once sang to my bride about this garden, and this is what I said to her: *I am come into my garden, my bride*[12] *(now in the place where he was crucified there was a garden*[13]*).* And what did you take from there? *I have gathered my myrhh.* For he drank wine mingled with myrhh and vinegar, and taking these he said: *It is finished.*[14] For the mystery is completed, the scriptures are fulfilled, sins are forgiven.

CYRIL OF JERUSALEM

IX

LOVE LOOKS AGAIN[1]

B UT MARY STOOD *weeping outside the tomb.*[2] Here we must ponder how strong a power of love had taken hold of the heart of this woman, who did not go away from the tomb of our Lord, even when the disciples did. She searched for him whom she had not found, and wept as she looked. Consumed with love for him, she longed for him who she believed had been taken away. And so it came about that only she, who stayed to look for him, saw him.

But, as she wept, Mary stooped and looked into the tomb. No doubt she had already seen it was empty, and had already made it known that the Lord was taken away. Why then did she bend down again? Why did she want to see once more? Simply because, for anyone who loves, it is not enough to have looked once, since love's power increases the determination to see. This is why the Church says of this very bridegroom in the *Song of Songs: Upon my bed by night I sought him whom my soul loves; I sought him, but found him not; I will rise now and go about the city, in the streets and in the squares; I will seek him whom my soul loves.*[3] For

we seek the Beloved on our bed when, in this present life, we
sigh with longing for our Redeemer in a little space of peace.
We look for him by night for, although our heart is already
awake to him, our eyes are still in the dark. Now, as we are
looking, the watchmen who keep the city find us. For
the holy Fathers who care for the estate of the Church meet
us in our holy concerns, to teach us either by word or by
writing. Scarcely have we passed them by when we find
him whom we love. For although our Redeemer was, in his
humility, a man among men, he was also above human beings in his divinity. So when the watchmen have gone by
the Beloved is found. For when we perceive that the
prophets and apostles are lower than he, we realize that he
who is by nature God is higher than human beings. And so he
is sought without being found so that later, when found,
he may be held the more securely. Holy desires increase by
being prolonged. If they diminish by delay, they were not
real desires. Anyone who makes contact with the truth burns
with this love. This is why David says: *My soul thirsts for
God, the living God. When shall I come and appear before
the face of God?*[4] And he urges us with the words: *Seek
his face evermore.*[5]

The angels inquired of Mary: *Woman why are you weeping?* And she said to them: *Because they have taken away my
Lord, and I do not know where they have laid him.*[6] Notice
that the account tells us that the woman did not say 'they
have taken away the body of my Lord', but 'they have taken
away my Lord.' *Saying this, she turned round and saw Jesus
standing, but she did not know that it was Jesus.* Because she
both loved and doubted, she saw and did not recognize him,
showed him her love while hiding her doubt.

*Supposing him to be the gardener, she said to him, Sir, if
you have carried him away, tell me where you have laid him,
and I will take him away.*[7] But how is it that, without telling
him for whom she was looking, and seeing him whom she
took for the gardener, she said: *Sir, if you have carried him*

away? The force of love often brings it about that we cannot believe that anyone does not know the one on whom our thoughts are always fixed. And so this woman does not say for whom she is looking, but says: *If you have carried him away.* For she cannot imagine that the person she mourns with ceaseless desire can be unknown to anyone else. *Jesus said to her, 'Mary'.*[8] It is as though our Lord clearly said: I do not know you in some general way, like everyone else, but specially. And so, because she is called 'Mary' by name, she recognizes her maker and at once calls him 'Rabboni', that is, 'Teacher'. For he it was who was outwardly sought and he who was inwardly teaching her to look for him.

GREGORY THE GREAT

X

THIS IS THE DAY[1]

*T*AKING AS OUR starting-point the words we have just sung to God, let us say what God gives us: *This is the day which the Lord has made.*[2]

These words, which are certainly prophetic, are meant to give us further understanding. What a very unusual day that must be which eyes of flesh never see. For it is not a day which dawns and dies, but a day which dawns and knows no setting!

Let us see what this same psalm says a little earlier: *The stone which the builders rejected has become the cornerstone. This is the Lord's doing, and it is wonderful in our eyes.*[3] And then there follows: *This is the day which the Lord has made.* Let us begin this day from the cornerstone.

Who is this cornerstone which the builders rejected if not our Lord Jesus Christ, whom the jewish doctors rejected? For the legal experts among the jewish doctors reproached him saying: *This man who breaks the sabbath does not come from God.*[4] The stone they rejected has become the cornerstone. Why is Christ called the cornerstone? Because every

cornerstone unites two walls coming from opposite direc-
tions. The apostles came from among the circumcised, they
came from the jewish people. There was another wall, the
Church that came from the gentiles. They met. There was
peace in Christ, unity in Christ, who made them both into
one building. He himself is the day which the Lord has made.
Understand by this the entire day, the head and the body,
This is the day which the Lord has made.

Remember the first beginnings of the world. *Darkness was
upon the face of the deep; and the Spirit of God was moving
over the face of the waters.* And God said: *Let there be light;
and there was light. And God separated the light from the
darkness. And he called the light day, and the darkness he
called light.*[5] Of this day the Apostle said: *Once you were
darkness, but now you are light in the Lord.*[6] Did he say
you were darkness in the Lord? No, there was darkness in
you, light in the Lord. But God called the light day, for by
his grace that was done which was done. For this is the day
which the Lord has made—not the day itself, but the Lord.

Was not Thomas a man, one of the disciples like any man
from the crowd? His fellow-disciples said to him: *We have
seen the Lord.*[7] And he said: Unless I touch, unless I place
my finger in his side. I will not believe. The evangelists bring
you the news, and you do not believe them? The world has
believed, and not the disciple? Of them it has been said:
*Their voice goes out through all the earth, and their words
to the ends of the world.*[8] Their words have gone out, they
have reached the ends of the earth, the whole world has
believed. Yet all the disciples tell one of their own, and he
does not believe. It was not yet the day which the Lord had
made. There was still darkness over the deep;[9] it was in the
depths of the human heart that the darkness was. Let him
come, let the beginning of that day come and say patiently,
not angrily, for he is a physician: I have come, he says,
I have come, touch and believe. You said: Unless I touch,
unless I put my finger, I will not believe. Come, touch,

put out your finger. I knew your wounds. I have kept my mark for you.

But evidently, stretching out his hand, he made his faith complete. For what is the fulness of faith? That we should believe Christ to be not only a man, nor believe him to be only God, but man and God. This is the fulness of faith. For, *the Word became flesh and dwelt among us.*[10] And so this disciple, to whom the Saviour offered the opportunity of touching his wounds and limbs, in touching cried out: *My Lord and my God.*[11] He touched a man and acknowledged God, he touched flesh and turned to the Word, for *the Word was made flesh and dwelt among us.*

> This Word let his flesh be hung on a tree,
> This Word let the nails be fastened in his flesh,
> This Word let his flesh be pierced by the lance,
> This Word let his flesh be laid in the tomb,
> This Word raised his flesh, showing himself
>   to be seen by his disciples,
>   offered himself to be touched by their hands.
> They touch and cry out: *My Lord and my God.*
>   *This is the day which the Lord has made.*

AUGUSTINE OF HIPPO

XI

SEEING WHAT WE EXPECT[1]

J HAVE DECIDED to discuss the general sense of today's gospel reading, and not each particular word, in case a longer exposition should be a burden to you. Now beloved, you have heard how to two disciples going on a journey our Lord appeared. Though not sure of him, they were talking about him, and he did not present them with an appearance they would recognize. Thus he did not fail to seem to their bodily eyes to be something that corresponded to what was going on in their hearts. For in their hearts they both loved and doubted. Yet the Lord was externally present to them, while not showing them who he was. In this way he showed his presence to them as they were speaking of him, yet in their doubting hid the form that would make him known. He addressed his words to them and reproached the insensibility of their understanding; he opened the mysteries of Holy Scripture concerning himself and yet, since he was still alien to their trust, he made as though he would go further. The simple Truth never does anything with duplicity, yet he showed himself to them in a bodily way exactly as he was in their minds. However, they were to be put to the test as to whether those who could not yet love him as God would at least care for him as a stranger. Yet since those with whom Truth went along could not be strangers to love, they invite him, as a stranger, to share their hospitality. Why do I say 'they invite' when it stands there that *they constrained him?*[2] From this it must surely be gathered that strangers are not simply to be offered hospitality, but actually pressed to it. A table is set, food is offered, and the God whom they had not known in the exposition of Holy Scripture, they recognized in the breaking of bread.

So, the commands of God are not made clear by hearing them, but by doing them. For it is written: *It is not the hearers of the law who are righteous before God, but the doers of the law.*[3] And so anyone who wishes to understand what he hears should be quick to put into practice what he can already understand. Notice that our Lord is not recognized when he is speaking, but consents to be known when he is being fed. And so, beloved, love hospitality, be devoted to the works of love. This is why it is said by the apostle Paul: *Let brotherly love continue. Do not neglect to show hospitality. For thereby some have entertained angels unawares.*[4]

GREGORY THE GREAT

XII

LOVE AGAIN YOUR OWN NATURE[1]

*A*ND SO, BELOVED, if we steadfastly believe in our hearts what we profess with our lips, we are crucified with Christ, dead with him, buried with him, and also risen with him on the third day itself. This is why the Apostle says: *If you have been raised with Christ, seek the things that are above, where Christ is, seated at the right hand of God. For when Christ who is your life appears, then you also will appear with him in glory.*[2] Now, that the hearts of the faithful may realize that, if they shun the desires of the world, they have within them the power to raise themselves to heavenly wisdom, our Lord promises his presence to us saying: *Lo, I am with you always, to the close of the age.*[3] For it was not in vain that the Holy Spirit said through the prophet Isaiah: *Behold, a virgin shall conceive and bear a son, and shall call his name Emmanuel, which means 'God with us'.*[4] Therefore Jesus fulfils the meaning of his name,

and he who ascends to heaven does not abandon those he has
adopted; he who sits at the right hand of the Father
likewise dwells there in his entire body, and he himself
strengthens with patience from above those whom he
invites to glory.

Let us then not be bewildered by the empty things around
us, or timid in the midst of difficulties. True, in the one
illusions present themselves, and in the other trials are heavy.
Yet because *the earth is full of the mercy of the Lord,*[5]
the victory of Christ is with us everywhere, in fulfilment of
his saying: *Do not be afraid; I have overcome the world.*[6]
And so, whether we struggle against worldly ambition, the
desires of the flesh, or the shafts of heretics, let us always
be armed with the cross of Christ. For we shall never be far
from the Easter festival if we abstain from the old leaven
of evil in the sincerity of truth.[7] Amid all the changes
of this life, which are full of different things to suffer,
we should always remember what the Apostle urges upon
us where he says: *Let this mind be in you, which was in
Christ Jesus who, though he was in the form of God, did not
count equality with God a thing to be grasped, but emptied
himself, taking the form of a servant, being born in the
likeness of men, and being found in human form he
humbled himself, becoming obedient unto death, even death
on a cross. Therefore God has highly exalted him and
bestowed on him the name which is above every name,
that at the name of Jesus every knee should bow, in
heaven and on earth and under the earth, and every
tongue confess that Jesus Christ is Lord to the glory of
the Father.*[8] If, he says, you understand the mystery of
this great love, and recall what the only-begotten Son of God
did for the salvation of human beings, then you have the
same thoughts that were in Christ Jesus, whose humility
no rich man could despise, no person of distinction blush
for. For human success could never raise us to such a
height that it would have reason to be ashamed of him who,

remaining in the form of God, did not think it unfitting to take on the form of a servant.

Imitate what he did; love what he loved and, finding the grace within you, love once again in him your own nature. For just as he did not lose his riches by his poverty, diminish his glory by his humility, or relinquish eternity by his death, so do you, following his path and walking in his steps, turn aside from earthly things to learn heavenly ones.

LEO THE GREAT

XII

ON THE SHORE[1]

*J*ESUS REVEALED HIMSELF *again to his disciples by the sea of Tiberias.*[2] We may ask why after his resurrection our Lord stood on the shore while the disciples were struggling on the sea when, before his resurrection, he had openly walked to them on the waves. The explanation of this is quickly understood if we consider the reason for it. For what does the sea symbolize if not this present world, which is beaten by the storms of circumstances and the waves of a changing life? And what is the firmness of the shore but the continuity of the repose of eternity? Because, then, the disciples were still involved in the waves of a mortal life, they were struggling at sea. But since our Redeemer had already passed beyond the decay of the flesh, after his resurrection he stood on the shore. It is as though, through physical images, he were speaking to his disciples of the mystery of his resurrection and saying: I no longer appear to you on the sea because I am no longer with you amid the waves of disturbance. This is why, in another place, after his resurrection he said to these same disciples: *These are the words I spoke to* *you while I was still with you.*[3]

We should also notice that our Lord is described as holding a final feast with his seven disciples—for Peter and Thomas, Nathanael, the sons of Zebedee, and two others of his disciples, are mentioned as being present. Why should he celebrate a final meal with seven disciples except to tell us in advance that only those who are filled with the sevenfold grace of the Holy Spirit will be with him in lasting refreshment. Further, in seven days all our times come into being, and completeness is often indicated by the number seven. And so those who here and now rise above earthly things in their eagerness for perfection feast at the final banquet on the presence of truth—those whom the love of this world does not bind, in whom, no matter what testing assaults against them it may make, it does not blunt the desires they have once conceived. Of that last banquet it is elsewhere said by John: *Blessed are those who are invited to the marriage supper of the Lamb.*[4] Thus those who are invited are not invited to breakfast but to supper, for evidently a banquet at the end of the day is supper. Those, then, when the time of this present life is over, who come to the refreshment of heavenly contemplation are invited, not to breakfast but to the supper of the Lamb. Now it is this supper which is depicted by the parting meal at which seven disciples are said to be present. For, as we have said, inner refreshment nourishes those who, filled with sevenfold grace, are athirst in the love of the Spirit. Let this be our case, brothers and sisters. Long to be filled with the presence of this Spirit. Consider what will follow you into the future from the present. Weigh well whether you are filled with this Spirit. For Paul proclaims what we have said with a genuinely sure word: *Anyone who does not have the spirit of Christ does not belong to him.*[5] It is as though he said: Anyone who is not ruled by God now dwelling in him, will not rejoice later in the vision of divine light. Yet in relation to what has been said we are weak, we have not yet reached the summit of perfection. We walk daily in the way of God with the steps of holy desire. Truth offers us comfort, when he says by the psalmist: *Your eyes have seen my imperfect being, and in your book all shall be written.*[6] Our imperfection will not do us any harm if in the way of God we do not look back to what is over, and press on to cover what remains. For he who is kind enough to give us the desires of the imperfect will one day strengthen us for perfection.

GREGORY THE GREAT

XIV

SITTING BESIDE THE FATHER[1]

JUST AS, AT THE EASTER festival, the resurrection of our Lord was the reason for our rejoicing, so his ascension into heaven is the subject of our joy today. We recall and celebrate as we should that day when, in Christ, our lowly nature was raised above the entire army of heaven, beyond all the orders of angels and the highest of the powers, to a seat beside that of God the Father. It is upon this succession of divine deeds that we are grounded and built up. The grace of God became more wonderful still when, although those things which were rightly felt to be worthy of its reverence were removed from human sight, still faith should not doubt, hope not waver, love not grow cold. For this is the strength of great souls, and this rather specially the light of believing spirits: to believe without hesitation things not seen by bodily sight, and to fix their desire where vision cannot come. For how could this devotion be born in our hearts, and how could we be justified by faith, if salvation consisted only in those things which fall beneath our gaze? This is why, to that man who seemed to doubt the resurrection of Christ unless he had examined by sight and touch the marks of his suffering body, our Lord said: *You believed because you saw me; blessed are they who have not seen and yet believed.*[2]

To make this happiness possible for us, my beloved, our Lord Jesus Christ, after completing everything that was appropriate to the teaching of the gospel and the mysteries of the New Testament, was raised to heaven on the fortieth day after his resurrection, putting an end to his bodily presence. He would remain at the right hand of the Father until the divinely appointed time for the adoption of the children of the Church was complete, and he would return to judge the living and the dead in that same flesh with which he ascended. And so what was visible about our Redeemer has now gone into the mysteries.[3] And that our faith might be nobler and firmer, there has followed upon sight a teaching whose authority is evident to the hearts of believers, enlightened by radiance from above.

Chains, prisons, exile, hunger, fire, the mawling of wild beasts, the terrible torments induced by the inhumanity of persecutors, cannot frighten this faith, which is increased by the ascension of our Lord, and strengthened by the gift of the Holy Spirit. This faith has cast out demons, driven away sickness, raised the dead. Hence, even the Apostles themselves who—in spite of being strengthened by so many miracles and instructed by so much teaching—had been filled with fear at the horror of our Lord's passion and, not without hesitation, had accepted the truth of his resurrection, profited so much by the ascension of our Lord that whatever had formerly made them afraid was turned into joy. And so let us rejoice, beloved, with spiritual joy and, happy in appropriate thanksgiving to God, let us freely raise our eyes to that place where Christ is. Let earthly desires not weigh down spirits that are summoned to raise themselves up.

LEO THE GREAT

XV

SOBER INTOXICATION[1]

*A*ND SO JESUS ASCENDED into the heavens, and kept his promise. For the Lord said: *Before many days you shall be baptized with the Holy Spirit.*[2] The grace is not given in any limited way, but its power is poured forth in all its fulness. For just as anyone, immersed in water at baptism, is literally surrounded by water, so were they completely baptized in the Spirit. Yet water surrounds us only externally, while the Spirit penetrates the soul and baptizes it completely.

And that the greatness of such a gift should not be unknown, something like a heavenly trumpet sounded. *For suddenly a sound came from heaven like the rush of a mighty wind,* as a sign of his gracious coming to those who would take the kingdom of heaven by violence, being visible in tongues of fire, and heard by its resonance. *And it filled the whole house where they were sitting.* The house became a vessel filled with the water of understanding. The disciples were sitting within it, and the whole house was filled. And so they were baptized completely, according to the promise, and clothed in soul and body with a heavenly and saving garment. And there appeared to them tongues of fire, distributed and resting upon each of them. *And they were all filled with the Holy Spirit and began to speak in other tongues as the Spirit gave them utterance.*[3]

The crowd of people who heard them was confused—a second confusion that was the exact opposite of the earlier and evil one at Babel. For there, the confusion of tongues was about fundamentals, since the intention was against God.[4] Here, there was a restoration of unity of thought, since the preoccupation was holy. What caused the fall was the very thing that brought about the restoration. They were amazed saying: How is it that we hear what they are saying? Do not be surprised if you do not understand. For Nicodemus also did not understand the coming of the Spirit, and he was told: *The wind blows where it wills and you hear the sound of it, but you do not know whence it comes or whither it goes.*[5] And if I, too, hear his voice, I do not know whence it comes—how shall I explain what he is in himself?

But others, mocking, said, they are filled with new wine.[6] Although in derision, they were in fact speaking the truth. For this was genuinely new wine—the grace of the New Testament. But this was new wine from a spiritual vine. It had often borne fruit in the prophets, and in the New Testament it sprouted anew. For as we know by experience, a vine can continue to be the same and, at different times, bear fruit according to the season. Likewise the Holy Spirit himself, remaining what he is, and often active in the prophets, has now shown us something new and wonderful. For grace had formerly come to the fathers, but now it overflows; then, they received a measure of the Holy Spirit. Now they are completely immersed in it.

But Peter having the Spirit, and knowing he had it said: *Men of Israel* who report Joel without understanding the Scriptures, *these men are not drunk as you suppose.*[7] They are indeed drunk, but not in the way you imagine. *They feast*

*on the abundance of your house, and you give them drink
from the river of your delights.*[8] They are drunk with that
sober intoxication[9] which is death to sin and life-giving
to the heart—quite the opposite of bodily drunkenness. For
that makes us forget even what we know. But this endows us
with a knowledge of things we did not know. They are drunk
by drinking the wine of the spiritual vine who says: *I am the
vine, you are the branches.*[10] And if you do not believe me,
then estimate what has been said by the time, *for it is the
third hour of the day.* As Mark says: *It was at the third hour
they crucified him.*[11] And now at the third hour he has sent
his grace. For that grace and this are not different. But he
who was crucified then, and promised this, has fulfilled what
he promised.

CYRIL OF JERUSALEM

XVI

JOY
TAKES OVER[1]

*J*N THE LIFE we are now living our thoughts ought habitually to return to the praise of God. For God's praise will be the endless joy of our life to come. And no one can become fit for that life who does not prepare himself for it now. This is why we praise God now; yet we also pray to him. Our praise has its portion of happiness, our prayer its sighs. For something we do not yet possess is promised to us. And since he who promised it is true,[2] we rejoice in hope;[3] but because we do not yet possess it, we sigh for it with longing.[4] It is good for us to persevere in this longing until what has been promised comes about. Then sighing ceases and joy takes over.

This is why there are two kinds of time: one which consists of the trials and troubles of this life now; the other which will be freedom from care and endless joy. A reminder of these two kinds of time is even prescribed for us—the one before Easter, and the other after. That which comes before Easter stands for the trouble in which we now find ourselves, while what we are at present celebrating after Easter implies something we do not yet possess. This is why we occupy the first time in fasting and prayer, but in this time when fasting is mitigated we give ourselves to praise. For this is the meaning of the *Alleluia* we sing which, as you know, is translated as *'Praise the Lord'*. So that other time comes before the resurrection, and this time after the resurrection of our Lord. At this time, the future life we do not yet possess is represented. For what we symbolize after our Lord's resurrection we shall possess after our own resurrection.

For in him who is our head, both times are prefigured, both displayed. The passion of our Lord shows us the unavoidable aspect of our present life. For we must work and be troubled and, in the end, die. But the resurrection and glorification of our Lord show us the life we are to receive.

And so, my brothers and sisters, I encourage you to praise the Lord. And this is what we all do when we say *alleluia.* *'Praise the Lord',* you say to your neighbour, and he says the same to you. When everyone encourages everyone else, they all do what is recommended. But you must praise God with your whole being. I mean, it is not only your tongue and your voice that must praise God, but your conscience too, your life, the things you do.

For we are now praising God while we are gathered together in church. But when each goes to his own home, it might seem that we cease to praise God. Let no one cease to live well, and then he will always praise God. You cease to praise God when you fall away from what is right and from what pleases him. For if you never fall away from the good life, then your tongue may be silent, but your life cries out, and the ears of God attend to your heart. For just as my ears hear your voices, so the ears of God hear our thoughts.

AUGUSTINE OF HIPPO

XVII

LIVING WATERS[1]

*L*ET US DRINK of living waters, welling up to eternal life. This our Saviour said about the Spirit which those who believed in him were to receive. Notice what he says: *Anyone who believes in me*—adding, *as Scripture says,* and sending you back to the Old Testament—*from within him shall flow rivers of living water.*[2] Not waters you can see, simply watering the earth that produces plants and trees, but bringing light to souls. And elsewhere he says: But the water that I shall give him will *become in him a spring of water welling up to eternal life.*[3] This is a new kind of water that lives and wells up—but springing from those who are worthy of it.

Why did he call the grace of the Holy Spirit water? Because water is of the substance of everything. Water produces green and living things. The water of the showers that come down from heaven falls as one thing, and produces many effects. Yet one source waters the whole of paradise; one and the same rain falls everywhere, and becomes white in the lily, red in the rose, purple in violets and hyacinths, and something different in all the different species. Thus in the palm-tree it is one thing, another in the vine, and everything in all. In itself it is one thing, and not other than itself. For the rain does not change and fall as this or that liquid but, adapting itself to the things that receive it, it becomes what is suitable to each. Likewise the Holy Spirit is one and indivisible, giving his grace to each one as he wishes. And just as a dry tree, when watered, puts out shoots, so the soul in sin, made worthy of the Holy Spirit by a change of heart, bears the fruits of justice. Though one in himself the Holy Spirit, by the desire of God and in the name of Christ, inspires many kinds of noble results. This one's tongue he guides in wisdom. He enlightens the soul of another with prophecy, to yet another he gives the power to cast out devils, to still another the gift of interpreting holy writ. One he confirms in continence, to another he teaches the works of mercy, he instructs another in fasting and mortification, another in detachment from bodily things, another he prepares for martyrdom—acting in different ways in different people, though he himself never varies.

His coming is gentle, his presence fragrant, his yoke light. Rays of light and knowledge anticipate his appearing. He comes with the feelings of a true guardian. For he comes to save and heal, to teach and correct, to strengthen and console, to give light to the mind—first to that of the one who receives him then, through him, to the mind of others. And just as someone, being at first in darkness and later getting a glimpse of the sun and receiving his sight, perceives what he did not see before, so the soul found worthy of the gift of the Holy Spirit is enlightened and sees, beyond human sight, what it did not know.

CYRIL OF JERUSALEM

XVIII

A NEW SONG[1]

WE ARE URGED to *sing to the Lord a new song.*[2] The new being knows the new song. The reason for the song is happiness and, if we ponder the matter carefully, its reality is love. And so anyone who understands how to love the new life knows how to sing the new song. For they all belong to the same world, the new being, the new song, the New Testament. And so the new being will both sing the new song and belong to the New Testament.

There is no one who does not love, but the question is what he loves. And so we are not urged not to love, but to choose what we love. And what shall we choose unless we are already chosen? For we never love unless we are first loved. Listen to the apostle John. He was the one who was lying close to the breast of the Lord and, at that supper, drinking in heavenly secrets. As a result of that draught and that happy intoxication he burst out with *In the beginning was the Word.*[3] High humility and sober intoxication! This great transmitter, this preacher, among the other things he imbibed from the Lord's breast also said this: *We love because he loved us first.*[4] For insofar as he was speaking of God, he allowed a lot to human beings when he said: *We love.* Who loves him? Human beings love God, mortals the undying One, sinners the just One, the unstable the changeless One, the made their Maker. And how does this come about? *Because he first loved us.* Inquire how a human being can love God and you will never find out, except because God loved them first. The one we love gave himself, gave our capacity to love. That what he gave is the source of our loving we learn more clearly from the Apostle Paul. *God's love,* he says, *has been poured into our hearts.* From where? From us, perhaps? No. From where then? *Through the Holy Spirit which has been given to us.*[5]

And so, having this great confidence, let us love God through God. Indeed, since the Holy Spirit is God, let us love God through God. Listen to that same John saying this more clearly: *God is love and anyone who abides in love abides in God, and God abides in him.*[6] It seems little enough to say: *Love is of God.* But which of us would go on to say: *God is love.* He said it who knew what he possessed.

I venture to say, my beloved, that we look among lesser things for something we find among higher ones. You do not see God. Love him and you possess him. How many things are loved with disreputable longings and not possessed! Many love and do not possess. They try to possess and mostly die before they find what they were looking for. God offers himself to us in the simplest way. He cries to us: Love me and you possess me, for you could not love me unless you possessed me.

Listen to me, holy and heavenly seed: *Sing to the Lord a new song.* Well, I am singing, you reply. Yes, you certainly are singing. I can hear you. But do not let your life bear witness against your tongue. Sing with your voice, sing with your heart. Sing with your lips, sing with your lives. *Sing to the Lord a new song.* Do you ask about his praise? *His praise is in the company of the saints.*[7] The praise to be sung is the singer. Do you wish to give God praise? Be what you say. You are his praise if you live rightly. *For anyone who loves evil hates his own soul.*[8]

AUGUSTINE OF HIPPO

XIX

SHINING
LIKE THE SUN[1]

AND SO *JESUS TOOK PETER and James and John, his brother, with him up a high mountain apart*[2] and showed them his glory, that the Apostles might with their whole heart receive the special strength of cheerful constancy, and not fear the difficulty of taking up the cross; and that they might not be ashamed of the sufferings of Christ or feel it dishonorable that, never losing the nobility of his power, he should undergo his passion with such patience. For although they understood the majesty of God in him, they did not yet know the power even of the body which concealed his divinity. This is why he promised in very express terms that there were some of his disciples who would not taste death until they had seen the Son of Man coming in his kingdom—that is to say, in royal splendor. He wanted it to be clear to these three men how special was the quality that pertained to the nature he had taken as human. For while they were clothed in mortal flesh, they could in no way behold and see that vision of the inex-

pressible and unapproachable Godhead which is reserved for
the pure of heart in eternal life.

Therefore, before chosen witnesses the Lord displayed his
glory, and that bodily form which he shares in common with
others shone with such splendour that his face was like the
sun in its brightness and his clothes like the white of the
snows. In this transfiguration what was chiefly intended was
that the scandal of the cross should be removed from the
hearts of the disciples, and that their faith should not be
disturbed by the humiliation of his voluntary passion once
the wonder of his hidden dignity had been revealed to them.
But by no less a providence the hope of holy Church was
given its foundation, that the whole body of Christ might
realize what kind of change would be given it, and that its
members might promise themselves a share in the privilege
which had shone forth in their head. About this matter this
same Lord had said when speaking of his coming in glory:
*Then will the righteous shine like the sun in the kingdom of
their Father.*[3] And the apostle Paul maintains the same when
he says: *I consider that the sufferings of this present time are
not worth comparing with the glory that is to be revealed in
us;*[4] and again: *You are dead and your life is hid with Christ
in God. When Christ, who is our life appears, then you also
will appear with him in glory.*[5]

LEO THE GREAT

XX

GOOD DAYS AND BAD[1]

*W*HENEVER WE HAVE TO ENDURE something that causes us anguish and difficulty, these things are meant both to caution us and also to set us right. For even our holy Scriptures themselves do not promise us peace, security, and quiet. The gospel is not silent about trials, difficulties, and causes of stumbling, *but anyone who endures to the end will be saved.*[2] For what that is good has this life ever offered since the time of the first man, the one who justly incurred death and suffered the curse from which our Lord Jesus Christ set us free?

And so, my brothers and sisters, we should not grumble *as some of them grumbled and were destroyed by serpents,* as the Apostle says.[3] What has the human race endured, my brothers and sisters, so unheard-of that our forefathers have not gone through something like it? When do we ever undergo such things as we know they underwent? Yet you find people complaining about their own times and saying how good were the times our parents knew. Would they also complain about their parents' time if they could call it back?

Do you not imagine that past times were good only because they were not *your* times, and that is why they are good?

But now that you are delivered from the curse, have believed in the Son of God, and are steeped and instructed in the holy Scriptures, it astonishes me that you can suppose that Adam had the best of good times. And your parents inherited Adam's burden. This is that Adam to whom it was said: *In the sweat of your face shall you eat bread and work the ground from which you were taken. Thorns and thistles shall it bring forth to you.*[4] This he incurred, this he suffered, this by the just decision of God was his lot. Why, then, do you imagine that past times were better than your own? From that Adam to the Adam who is today, it has been all toil and sweat, thorns and thistles. Has the flood escaped our notice, and the distressing times of famine and war that are described in Scripture in case we should murmur against God about our own times? Who is equal to describing the wars and hunger of those days? What really terrible times they were! Are we not all horrified at what we have heard and read about them? This is to give us something to be grateful for, instead of grumbling about our own times.

AUGUSTINE OF HIPPO

BIOGRAPHICAL NOTES ON THE AUTHORS

ORIGEN   Most probably born in Alexandria about the
year 185, Origen became so great a man that
even those who find him uncongenial can scarcely deny the
boldness of his enterprises, the unusual learning he brought
to them, or the devotion to the Church which inspired all he
did. As a young man he was put in charge of the catechumens
in Alexandria and in 230 ordained a priest in Palestine. Much
of his huge output has not survived, and some of it only in
latin translation, because of the criticism that was brought to
bear on it and on him personally, mostly after his death. His
was, to some extent, the fate of the gifted pioneer. But
St Gregory Thaumaturgus has left us a description of the
excitement of being a young pupil of his, and St Jerome was
able to draw on the resources he left for the study of the text
of the Old Testament. As a fine old patristic scholar, Canon
Geoffrey Prestige, said of him, many years ago in a memor-
able lecture: 'It may seem astonishing that he has never been
canonised, for in addition to supreme services to Christianity
he lived a confessor and died, to all intents, a martyr'.[1] After
years of teaching, preaching and writing, he was captured
and cruelly tortured under the persecution of the emperor
Decius and died as a result of his injuries at Tyre in 253-4 in
his sixty-ninth or seventieth year.

---

1. *Fathers and Heretics* (London: SPCK, 1940) 43.

LEO I, 'THE GREAT'   Of the early life of Leo, who may perhaps have been born in Tuscany about the year 400, we know relatively little. Although his writings show some direct influence of North African writers, especially Augustine, his substantial formation was evidently that of the old catechetical school in Rome, where we first hear of him as a deacon. He was elected to the see of Rome in the year 440 while absent on a diplomatic mission in Gaul, as he mentions in the first sermon he preached on his return on 29 September of that same year. Although he knew no Greek, he was to be venerated as much by the East as the West on account of a letter (Epistle 28) written to the Patriarch Flavian of Constantinople on 13 June 449. The doctrine of this letter on the person of Christ was accepted by the Council of Chalcedon (451) as a standard of Christian orthodoxy. This *Flavian Tome,* as it came to be called, taught that Jesus Christ, the Divine Word, unites in his one person the two natures, human and divine, unconfused and unmixed, though communicating with each other while retaining their particular faculties. Thus it is true to say that the Son of God died on the cross. Leo's sermons, of which we have ninety-six, were written in a distinctive latin rhythmic prose of great concision, the full effects of which it would be impossible to convey in translation into English, a language which has virtues of another kind, though either language is capable of its own clarity. And for all his art Leo is both simple and clear. Among the Greeks Leo is remembered on 18th February, while in the revised calendar of the Roman Church he is now remembered on the day of his death, 10 November 461.

GREGORY I, 'THE GREAT'   The only other pope, than Leo I, to be given the honorific title 'Great', as they are also the only two early popes of whose reigns we have a collection of letters which mirror their activities in the service of the Church. Gregory leads us to suppose that he was born in Rome a little before 540. His father was a senator, and he himself had become prefect of the city, the highest magistrate in Rome, before 573. These years of experience were to be important for him later when many responsibilities fell upon him. Not without hesitation, he became a monk, founding a monastery dedicated to St Andrew in his father's house in Rome, and six others on family properties in Sicily. Ordained deacon in 579, he was sent as papal representative to the Emperor Maurice in Constantinople, where in the company of other monks from St Andrew he remained for six years, returning to Rome to live the monastic life there about 585-6. On 3 September 590, after six months of reluctance, he finally accepted ordination as pope in succession to his predecessor in the see, who had died of the plague at the beginning of that year. Of a sensitive disposition, and suffering increasingly from a disabling stomach complaint, he devoted himself unremittingly to pastoral interests, and the motive behind all his writings is ultimately pastoral. His voluminous reflections on the book of Job, like his other writings on Scripture, were originally addressed to a monastic audience. For his clerics he wrote a book on pastoral care which was much in use in later centuries and first translated into English by King Alfred. His *Dialogues,* a collection of folk-tales about holy men, including our only materials for the life of St Benedict, were aimed at devout lay-folk. In a greek translation by pope Zachary they earned him in the East the title of 'dialogist'. The group of forty homilies he had written in the years 590-593 also envisaged a wide popular audience. The first twenty of these, with the exception of number seventeen, were read for him by a secretary as he was himself sometimes unable to speak for stomach pain. But the final twenty he was able to deliver himself. These homilies with many attractive and distinctive insights were understandably much read in later centuries. The importance of his work as an analyst of the spiritual and ascetic life can scarcely be exaggerated. After a full and devoted life he died 11 March 604. The revised roman calendar has now moved his feast from the March date to that of his ordination in September.

AUGUSTINE OF HIPPO   Augustine was born on 13 November 354 at Thagaste in North Africa, the modern Souk Ahras in Algeria, and it is reasonable to suppose that he was of pure Berber stock. But it is important to realize that the North Africa of his day was and had been for more than two centuries latin in culture and language. A citizen of the late Roman Empire, Augustine was born of a poor father and had none of the family advantages of a man like St Ambrose who was to baptize him in 386 in Milan, where the young and ambitious Augustine had gone to gain by education what he lacked by birthright. In him so many of the currents affecting the Christianity of late antiquity meet in a rich and reflective personality. In his *Confessions* Augustine ponders in the presence of God the different factors which have shaped his life and development, and he does so in a way which anticipates approaches to personal life that still make him come close to his readers. Reviewing his many books in his old age, Augustine was able to say of this product of his middle age, written in 397 (two years after he had been made bishop of Hippo), that it continued to move even him as it had when he was writing it. When he died on 28 August 430, he had still been unable to review among the vast production of a lifetime many of those sermons of which at least texts from the hand of stenographers existed from among the many more he must have preached when, at times, he was preaching to his people daily. For reasons given in the notes it has seemed convenient to choose here examples from two of the great series on the gospel of John and on the psalms, and it is hoped that all the choices will reveal aspects of Augustine unsuspected by those who know him by the often derogatory remarks made about him at second or third hand by people who never read him.

Anyone who wishes to form a more lively impression of Augustine's entire life as writer, thinker and bishop would do well to turn to the fine biography of Peter Brown, *Augustine, of Hippo* (London, 1969), which is itself constantly informed by wide reading in Augustine. On a much smaller scale, but also of reliability and distinction, is H. Marrou, *St Augustine* in the *Men of Wisdom* series, originally in French but translated into English (London, 1957). Readers fortunate enough to have access to the *Confessions* in the Penguin Classics Series by R.S. Pine Coffin will find themselves in the hands of a translator of unusual gifts.

CYRIL OF JERUSALEM　Like Leo at a later date, Cyril emerges as a product of a catechetical school—in this case Jerusalem, where he was probably born about 315. Raised to the diaconate by bishop Maximus of Jerusalem, he was a priest in or after 342 and eventually, in 348, bishop. He was banished three times from his see, but appears to have played a significant role at the First Council of Constantinople in 381. His reputation rests largely on a remarkable series of twenty-four baptismal catecheses, of which only the pre-baptismal ones are quoted here. There are manuscript indications that what we have is a stenographer's report of what was evidently lively instruction. The series is difficult to date, but somewhere about the Lent and Easter of 350 is commonly suggested. Cyril died on 18 March 386, the day on which he is remembered in both East and West.

NOTES

INTRODUCTION

It should be remembered that the Fathers had no modern critical texts of Scripture, and often quote or adapt from memory, so that scriptural quotations will not always correspond exactly with the texts of references given in modern bibles. This is particularly true of quotations from the psalms, where there is sometimes still real doubt about the meaning of the Hebrew. In addition, the Fathers and early liturgies numbered the psalms themselves, and the verses within them, according to the Greek Septuagint or Old Latin Psalter, the verse numbering including the old 'titles' of the psalms. In these notes the old reference is given first with the Hebrew and modern equivalent in brackets. All the passages in this anthology have been translated by the author from the original latin or greek texts as indicated in the individual notes. For convenience the following conventional abbreviations have been used:

CCL   *Corpus Christianorum, Series Latina*
PG   J.P. Migne, *Patrologiae Cursus Completus, Series Graeca*
PL   J.P. Migne, *Patrologiae Cursus Completus, Series Latina*
SCh   *Sources Chrétiennes*

I REBECCA AT THE WELL

1. This is paragraph two and the opening of three, with its final sentence, from the tenth of Origen's homilies on Genesis, written when he was in his sixties. The text used here is that of SCh 7bis (Paris, 1976), which is substantially that of the 1920 edition of W. Baehrens.

2. Cf. Gen 24:13. A grasp of Genesis 24 as a whole is necessary for understanding many of the allusions in this homily.

3. Cf. Gal 4:23.
4. Gen 24:22.
5. Hos 2:19-20.
6. Rom 1:14
7. Gen 24:14.
8. Mt 25:35.
9. Cf. Jn 7:38.
10. Jn 4:7.
11. Amos 8:11.
12. Jn 7:37.
13. Cf. Mt 5:6

14. Ps 41:2-3 (42:1-2).
15. Cf. Gen 24:62-63.

II AFTER HIS IMAGE

1. These are the two opening paragraphs of the first of the sermons of Leo for the ember days of December, preached on 17 December 450. The latin text is that of PL 54 (Sermon XII), also reprinted in SCh 200:150-156. The thought begins from the text of Gen 1:26-27.

2. Although not a direct quotation from Scripture, this and similar lapidary formulas found in Leo and other Fathers are heavily dependent on the thought of phrases like 1 Cor 15:22.

3. Is 42:16.

4. Is 65:1.

5. 1 Jn 5:20, 4:19.

6. Leo is here partly quoting, partly alluding to Sallust: *Idem velle atque idem nolle ea demum firma amicitia est* (To choose and refuse the same things is, in the long run, solid friendship). *De conjuratione Catalinae* 20.4.

7. Ps 29:6 (30:5). Only the Latin gives Leo's sense.

8. Deut 6:5, Lev 19:18.

9. Acts 14:16-17.

10. Phil 2:10-11.

III CLAIMING OUR HONOUR

1. The whole of the final paragraph of Gregory's homily eight on the Gospel, intended for Christmas Day (PL 76:1104C-1105B).

2. Lk 2:14 (the Vulgate and Old Latin liturgical reading).

3. Rev 22:9.

4. A reference to Ps 81:6 (82:6), cited by our Lord himself in Jn 10:13: *Is it not written in your law, 'I said you are gods'?*

IV LIGHTS IN THE WORLD

1. The substance of the arguments of paragraphs three and four of the fifth of Leo's sermons for the Epiphany (sermon XXXV; PL 74; SCh 22bis: 258-264).

2. Rom 8:17.

3. Mt 11:28-30.

4. 1 Cor 6:20, Phil 2:15.

5. Eph 5:8.

6. Mt 5:16.

V LAZARUS, COME OUT!

1. The substance of paragraphs two, seven, eight, and ten of Augustine's homily twenty-two on the Gospel of John, preached on 28 July 413 (CCL 36:223-4, 227, 228-229, or PL 35:1575-1579). This homily deserves its place here, both in its own right and as representing the symbolic significance attached to the raising of Lazarus, to which catacomb iconography and the continuous tradition of icon painting bears witness from the earliest christian times.

2. Jn 5:24.
3. Jn 1:1.
4. Jn 5:25.
5. An allusion to Jas 2:19.
6. 1 Jn 2:18.
7. Jn 14:6.
8. Eph 5:8.
9. Jn 5:26.

VI FRIENDS OF GOD

1. The entire text of the first three paragraphs of Gregory's influential homily twenty-seven, preached in the basilica of the martyr St Pancras on his feast day. The fourth paragraph is also entire at the beginning, but the concluding phrases are a careful conflation of Gregory's own words on the martyrs as witnesses to the truth (PL 76: 1205A-1206B). In the second half of this homily, not translated here, Gregory expresses his concern for those who have come to the celebration with very unchristian petitions on their lips. He warns them that God sees unforgiving hearts and will not listen to them.

2. The homily is in effect a concentrated reflection on the text of Jn 15:12-16.
3. Lk 23:34.
4. Jn 15:13.
5. 1 Jn 3:17.
6. Lk 3:11.
7. Jn 15:14-15.
8. An expression unique in Gregory's writing, apparently identifying love and knowledge. It was to be important for twelfth-century writers, notably St Bernard who cites this phrase and Gregory by name in his sermon *De diversis* 29.1 (PL 183:620C). There can be little doubt that in the thought of Gregory it is our authentic love of God that leads us ultimately to the vision of divine things and that, in conformity with this view, he allows that a great love of what has been promised may in a certain sense give an anticipation in this world

of what is not yet seen.

9. This phrase is the Old Latin rendering of Ps 138:17 (139:16) and was much quoted in relation to the apostles in patristic and medieval writers and the liturgy. The revised Vatican psalter, like the Coverdale and all modern psalters, translates the key hebrew word as 'thoughts' rather than 'friends'.

10. Gregory is evidently quoting the phrase about friends as 'soul-keepers' from the *Etymologies* of St Isidore of Seville (10:4; PL 81: 567). On the other hand it is perhaps likely that Aelred of Rievaulx, who quotes it in his work on *Spiritual Friendship* (PL 195:663C), was led to it through Gregory.

VII THE CHRIST OF THE PSALMS

1. Another example from a great series of Augustine covering the entire psalter and put together over a period of years from 392-418. It gives us an articulate view of the christian and patristic use of the psalter as an inspired prayer-book of the Church. These paragraphs from the explanation of Ps 140 (141) sketch in the simplest form the notion of Christ speaking in the psalter, as it were, with two voices, the personal and the representative. This translation gives us the conclusion of paragraph three, with the exception of a few lines, the whole of paragraphs four and five and most of the latter half of twenty-five (CCL 40:2027-2029, 2044; PL 37:1817-1818, 1831-1832).

2. 1 Cor 12:27.

3. Mt 19:5.

4. Ps 140:1 (141:1).

5. The sweat 'like drops of blood' is only recorded in some ancient authorities for the gospel of Luke (Lk 22:43-44, cf. RSV note).

6. Ps 140:2 (141:2).

7. Rom 6:6.

8. Ps 21:2 (22:1), Mt 27:46 ≅ Mk 15:34.

9. This is the meaning of the Old Latin of the last phrase of Ps 140: 10 (141:10). The Hebrew is, in any case, a little awkward to construe, and Augustine's latin text suggests to him an appropriate occasion to make this a commentary on the complete mystery of the passion and resurrection in its application to the christian soul.

10. Jn 13:1.

11. Jn 12:24, 32.

VIII FELLOW-TRAVELLERS

1. The first lines of paragraph one with the conclusion of four, followed by the whole of thirty and thirty-one and the opening phrases

of thirty-two of Cyril's Catechesis XIII (PG 33:772,778, 808-812).

2. Is 53:12 quoted in Mk 15:28 and Lk 22:7.
3. Ps 108:25 (109:24).
4. Lk 23:42.
5. Lk 23:43.
6. Ps 94:8 (95:7-8).
7. Gen 2:17.
8. Rom 5:20.
9. Cf. Mt 20:1-6.
10. Mt 20:13,15.
11. Ps 118:176 (119:176).
12. Sg 5:1.
13. Jn 19:41.
14. Jn 19:30.

IX LOVE LOOKS AGAIN

1. Gregory's homily twenty-five on the Gospel, preached on the Thursday after Easter in the Lateran basilica, the old church of the popes, is a prolonged meditation on the text of Jn 20:11-18. The translation beginning in the middle of paragraph one continues through almost the whole of two with the substance of four and five. (PL:1189B-1190D, 1191D-1193A).
2. Jn 20:11.
3. Sg 3:1-2.
4. Ps 41:3 (42:2).
5. Ps 104:4 (105:4).
6. Jn 20:13.
7. Jn 20:15.
8. Jn 20:16.

X THIS IS THE DAY

1. By way of commentary on a phrase from the psalms in constant use at Easter since early times, Augustine brings together the idea of Christ as cornerstone of the Church and as the light of the day of the new creation. With the exception of a few phrases from paragraphs one and three, this is his Easter sermon 258 entire (SCh 116:344-350).
2. Ps 117:24 (118:24).
3. Ps 117:22-23 (118:22-23). Quoted by Jesus (Lk 20:17) and in 1 Pet 2:7.
4. Jn 9:16.
5. Gen 1:2-5.
6. Eph 5:8

7.   Jn 20:25.
8.   Ps 18:5 (19:4).
9.   Gen 1:2.
10. Jn 1:14.
11. Jn 20:28.

XI SEEING WHAT WE EXPECT

1.   Gregory's short homily twenty-three on the gospel, preached in St Peter's basilica on Easter Monday, is a weekday meditation on the resurrection story of Lk 24:13-25. It concludes with one of Gregory's own folk tales (not translated here) about an habitually hospitable householder whose guest disappears as he turns in his service, and who tells him in a dream that whatever is done for the least of his brethren is done for their Lord. (PL 176:1182B-1183A)
2.   Lk 24:29.
3.   Rom 2:13.
4.   Heb 13:1-2.

XII LOVE AGAIN YOUR OWN NATURE

1.   This is paragraphs three, four and the opening lines of five of Leo's second Easter sermon. (sermon 72; PL 54; SCh 74:131-132)
2.   Col 3:1 & 4.
3.   Mt 28:20.
4.   Is 7:14.
5.   Ps 32:5 (33:5).
6.   Jn 16:33.
7.   Cf. 1 Cor 5:8.
8.   Phil 2:5-8.

XIII ON THE SHORE

1.   Gregory's homily twenty-four on the Gospel will perhaps seem to some to carry a symbolic interpretation of Jn 21:1-14 almost unpardonably far, yet there are unmistakable signs in the text of the Gospel itself that a high degree of symbolism is intended. The translation gives the substance of paragraphs two and six. (PL 176:1184D-1185A, 1187C-1188C)
2.   Jn 21:1.
3.   Lk 24:44.
4.   Rev 19:9.
5.   Rom 8:9.
6.   Ps 138:16 (139:15)

XIV SITTING BESIDE THE WATER

1.   Leo's second sermon for the ascension of our Lord is of considerable theological and liturgical importance. The translation gives the second half of paragraph one, the whole of two, and the opening lines of three and five. (sermon 74; PL 54 or SCh 74:139-141, 142-143)

2.   Jn 20:29.

3.   *in sacramenta transivit* is Leo's latin phrase. It seems preferable to keep the word 'mysteries' in translating this, for although it is tolerably certain that Leo is thinking of the presence of Christ in what would later be called 'the sacraments' in the narrower sense, it seems unlikely that he wishes to *confine* himself to them. It is perhaps preferable to say, by reference to Leo's firm conviction of the truth of the Incarnation, that the visible presence of Christ by his human birth establishes the sacramental principal and that, after his ascension, it is, as it were, 'natural' that he should be present to us in mysteries.

XV SOBER INTOXICATION

1.   This translation attempts to give an impression of Cyril's lengthy catechesis seventeen using only his own words from paragraph thirteen to nineteen, concluding in the middle of that paragraph. (PG 33: 985-991)

2.   Acts 1:5.

3.   Acts 2:2-4.

4.   Cf. Gen 11:1-9.

5.   Jn 3:8.

6.   Acts 2:13.

7.   This is equivalently a quotation from Acts 2:15-16.

8.   Ps 35:9 (36:8).

9.   The notion of 'sober intoxication' which evidently derives from the description of the effects of the coming of the Holy Spirit in the Acts, occurs among both Greek and Latin writers of patristic times, and in some of the older liturgical hymns. Another example of it in Augustine, writing in Latin, will be found in the second paragraph of XVIII in this anthology. All writers who use it wish to suggest the combination of spiritual light in the mind and warmth in the heart with complete lucidity of vision and understanding.

10.   Jn 15:5.

11.   Acts 2:15, Mk 15:25. It is, of course, for this reason that the old liturgical prayer of terce, said at 9 AM, is associated with prayer to the Holy Spirit.

XVI JOY TAKES OVER

1.   The first paragraph and the beginning of the second from a sermon of Augustine to his people at Hippo on Psalm 148 (CCL 40:
2165-2166 or PL 38:1937-1938).

2.   Heb 10:23.

3.   Rom 5:2.

4.   The thought of this sentence is heavily dependent on the argu-
ment of Rom 8:18-25.

XVII LIVING WATERS

1.   This passage gives in Cyril's own words the substance of the
middle section of Cyril's catechesis sixteen, paragraphs eleven, twelve,
and sixteen (PG 33:932-936, 940-941).

2.   Jn 7:38,39.

3.   Jn 4:14.

XVIII A NEW SONG

1.   An undated sermon of Augustine preached at Carthage. The
translation gives the beginning and paragraph two with the substance of
paragraphs three–six and the final sentence of eight (CCL 41:424-427).

2.   Ps 149:1.

3.   Jn 1:1.

4.   1 Jn 4:10 (The Latin has the word 'first', which is the sense of
the text).

5.   Rom 5:5.

6.   1 Jn 4:16.

7.   Ps 149:1, the second phrase in the verse.

8.   Ps 10:6 Vulgate only and much quoted. For this second phrase of
Ps 11:5 the Coverdale and all modern psalters render the Hebrew as
meaning that it is God who hates those who love evil.

XIX SHINING LIKE THE SUN

1.   Of this Archbishop Michael Ramsey has said: 'Amongst all the
patristic literature which refers to the Transfiguration a place of honor
perhaps belongs to the sermon of Pope Leo devoted to the event.
Preached on the Ember Saturday in Lent upon the gospel for the day,
it gathers up nearly every aspect of the theology of the Transfiguration
and presents it with a striking lucidity and vigour and with a practical
bearing upon the Christian Life' (*The Glory of God and the Transfiguration of Christ*, 1967 edn., p. 133). This translation begins with
the last lines of paragraph two and concludes with the whole of three

For the sake of comprehension in English it seemed necessary to invert the order of the first sentence (sermon 51; PL 54 or SCh 74:16-18).

2.   Mt 17:1.
3.   Mt 13:43.
4.   Rom 8:18.
5.   Col 3:3-4.

XX GOOD DAYS AND BAD

1.   This is the striking first paragraph of a sermon by Augustine printed in the *Supplement* to the latin Migne, ed. A. Hammon, vol 2, col 441-442. The second paragraph, not translated here, returns to a theme dear to Augustine, the longing for eternity which the fleeting and incomplete nature of time inspires.

2.   Mt 10:22.
3.   1 Cor 10:9-10.
4.   Gen 3:18-19.

ACKNOWLEDGEMENTS

With the single exception of the pleasant verse applied to the Fathers in the introductory pages (Ps 91:15 [92:13]) from the English of the Grail Psalter, it has seemed best to translate the psalms which occur in this anthology according to their sense in the passages concerned. In other quotations from scripture the Revised Standard version has been used to the extent that it seemed possible but, for the reasons given in the explanation of the notes, not always consistently. For the rest I must owe a lot to the many translations I have read since I first became fascinated by the Fathers as a schoolboy, though I am not aware of any conscious borrowing. In any case I must owe at least as much to those who have encouraged and commented on my work over the years in my efforts to make the Fathers better understood and appreciated. To them especially this small collection is offered as a token from among the many translations I am unlikely ever to have the leisure to revise.

Father Joseph Fessio SJ of the St Ignatius Institute in the University of San Francisco kindly arranged for me to have a long loan of the text of Cyril of Jerusalem in PG 33. Otherwise, in the immediate compilation of this little book my prior, Dom Bruno Barnhart, has given me the discreet and practical support that those who know him would expect, while the youngest member of my community, Brother Cassian Hardie, has both anticipated a number of my human needs and filled some of the many gaps I might otherwise have left in my regular duties about the house. Finally, my editor, Dr Rozanne Elder, has shown me a lot of the patience with details that only those with experience in the proper compilation of books really understand. Any faults that remain must be my own.

§

When you walk through fire, the flame shall not burn you,
for I am the Lord your God (Is 43:2-3). And so every situa-
tion makes room for the upright, and everything that is made
renders its fitting service. And do not suppose that these
things which happened in former times have no bearing upon
what happens to you, who hear about them now. For they
shall be accomplished for you in a spiritual way.

(Origen on Joshua, homily 4.1)